O Lord
Where is the God
Who loves me?

My faltering one
Where is the child
Who trusts me?

Lord, Don't You Love Me Anymore?

RUTH HARMS CALKIN

LIVING BOOKS
Tyndale House Publishers, Inc.
Wheaton, Illinois

Interior illustration by Marla Shega

First printing, July 1988
Library of Congress Catalog
Card Number 88-50389
ISBN 0-8423-3827-6
Printed in the United States of America

To

Maureen Brians

My cherished friend

From whom I have learned so much

Of God's consistent love

CONTENTS

A God
Who Loves

EVERLASTING LOVE

He is seven years old
And he's my friend.
His eyes are merry, his hair is short
His nose is covered with freckles.
On a cold, rainy day we sat on the floor
Eating hot buttered popcorn.
The popcorn went down quickly,
But the questions came out slowly.

"If I told a lie today, would God stop loving me?"
"No, of course not, David."
"What if I told two lies, or three
Would He stop loving me then?"
"No, but you'd be unhappy in your heart."
"What if I punched Johnnie in the nose
And made his nose bleed—*hard?*
Would God stop loving me then?"
"No, but you better not try it."
"What if I threw a rock and broke your
    window?
Would God stop loving me then?"
"No, but you'd have to work hard to pay for it."
"What if I stepped on the snails
That ate all your flowers?
Would God stop loving me then?"
"Not for a minute, David."
"When would God ever stop loving me?"
"David, not until there is no more earth
And no more heaven

And no more love
And no more God."
"Then it's never going to happen
No matter what."
"That's right, David.
Even if it sometimes *feels* like it might
It's never going to happen
No matter what."

I have loved you, O my people, with an everlasting love . . . (Jer. 31:3, TLB).

THE PRAYER

For so many anguished months
I've been waiting for You to answer
The one longing desire of my heart.
I've begged, pleaded, agonized.
I've prayed at times fumblingly
At other times intensely.
I've knelt and prayed.
I've buried my head in my pillow and prayed.
I've prayed before breakfast
And after lunch.
I've prayed before dawn
And after dark.
I've prayed with spontaneous outbursts
While tears washed my face.
I've prayed over our kitchen sink
And as I shopped for groceries.
I've prayed amid screeching traffic.
At times I've prayed with confidence
At other times with fear.
And yet, Lord, though I have waited
Though I have strained to listen
There is no answer.
I hear nothing . . . just nothing.
O God, I am so puzzled, so bewildered.
A frightening thought haunts me.
Could it be true, Lord?
Don't You love me anymore?

My child
Because I love you so much
I wait for you to let Me
Remove the harmful desire.

THE CALENDAR

God, there are some years
We would like to cross off the calendar.
This is one of those years.
From January to December my husband and I
Have felt like wounded soldiers
Fighting a losing battle.
Hospitals, life-threatening illness
Surgeries, financial drain, pain
A family death, grief, anxiety
Night-tossing, weariness, silent tears.
Other things, too:
A flooded patio, pieces of roofing
Scattered by howling winds
Two car accidents in bumper-to-bumper traffic
Dwindling hope, thundering doubts
The fear-stabbing question
"Lord, don't You love us anymore?"

And yet, dear God
How dare we deny Your day-by-day comfort
At times when we needed it most,
Phone calls bringing encouragement, notes in the
    mail
Delicious meals lovingly prepared by friends
A paragraph in a book renewing our trust
Your Word bringing light in the darkness
A sparrow's song during drizzling rain
Your whispered words to our hearts:
"When the pain stays, I stay, too."

O God, You have been our high tower
You have been our hiding place
You have been our sure defense.
The hymn of the Psalmist is our hymn, too:
"I will bless the holy Name of God
And not forget the glorious things He does."
Over this year's calendar we will finally write
"Surely the Lord was in this place
Though we knew it not."

YOU LOVE ME

God
When I am wretched and weak
You love me.
When I am steady and strong
You love me.
When I am very right
Or terribly wrong
You love me.
When I talk too much
Or laugh too loud
Or sob too long
You love me.
When I am quiet and serene
You love me.
When I willingly obey
You love me.
When I insist on my own way
You love me.
When I fail to put You first
You love me.
When I come running back to You
You love me.
I need not beg You to love me
For You who are Love
Cannot exist without loving.

And yet this very day, dear God
I have no real assurance

Of Your love at all.
I wonder why?

Beloved child
The fact remains:
I love you.

THE LIVING GOD

I place my whole confidence
In the Living God.
Not because things
Are going my way.
Not because I have what I want.
Not because I understand
All the inexplainables
Or because I am immune
To problems and pain and sorrow.
But despite my questions
My reversals, my disappointments
Despite my sorrow and tears
I place my whole confidence
In the Living God
For He alone can see me through.
He alone is worthy of my trust.

BEAUTIFUL THINGS HAPPEN

O God
Such beautiful things happen
When I meet You day by day
In quietness and confidence.
There is a deep inner wholeness
And the assurance of Your guidance.
I am not so easily disturbed
By changing circumstances.
I am less dependent on others
And more dependent on You.
My eyes may be full of tears
But my heart is full of joy.
In discovering Your hidden treasures
I learn how deeply I am treasured by You.
When day by day I am responsive
To Your whispered secrets
You do more for me in one day
Than I could do for myself in a lifetime.

ALWAYS THERE

So often, Lord
I reach the bottom of the abyss.
So often I taste the dregs
Of my own helplessness.
Yet it is there, *exactly there*
That You come to my immediate rescue.
When I feel totally impoverished
Of all self-sufficiency
When I want to vanish into nowhere
From the depths of despair
I call Your Name
And You are always there for me!

IRREVERSIBLE YES

God, You have done
A beautiful thing for me.
You have freed me from the dissatisfaction
Of so many empty days and months.
Into my impoverished heart
You have poured life-changing thoughts of You
Making each new day gloriously rich.
You have struck a deep artesian well in my soul
As sheer joy springs forth.
All because in an act of honest surrender
When life had lost its challenge
I said an irreversible YES to You!

AT LAST

At last there is One
With whom I am perfectly safe.
One who knows thoroughly
All the rubbled ruins of my heart.
At last I see that all that is
Riddled and distorted in me
Can still find God-planned fulfillment.
At last I need no longer explore
The deep, dark forest of my thoughts
For there is One who understands me
Far better than I understand myself.
One who stands with me
In the thick of the battle
One who supports me
On the slippery, ice-crested paths.
At last I have entrusted myself
To One who guarantees my wholeness
Someone whose love is immeasurable.
In all the world He alone can love me
As I need to be loved.
At last there is One—
My Lord and my God!

MY GLORIOUS ENOUGH

Oh, how I love You, my Lord
But not enough.
How I hunger and thirst for You
But not enough.
How I rejoice in Your inimitable goodness
But not enough.
Pour Yourself lavishly, dear God
Into every vacant hollow
Into every cluttered chamber
Of my longing heart.
Free me from every shallow substitute
From every hidden pretense
Until I shall know
With deep, consuming conviction
That You are my Glorious Enough.

THE PROMISE

God, on a long, lonely Saturday
Just before New Year's Day
You spoke so clearly through Your Word:
"Your days of mourning all will end.
You will live in joy and peace."
O God, what a glorious promise
As we begin a brand new year!
Again You said:
"Always be expecting much
From Him, your God."
I trust You implicitly, my Lord
For Your "much" exceeds by far
My greatest comprehension of much.
Surely You have planned a beautiful surprise!
I open my heart wide to receive it.

GOD, HOLD ME CLOSE

O God
Hold me close
While I cry
For my freedom.

The louder I shout
The deeper my soul
Needs to know

You will never, never
Let me go.

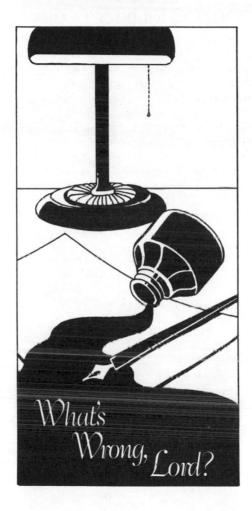

What's Wrong, Lord?

WHAT'S WRONG, LORD?

I am alone, Lord
So alone.
You no longer walk with me.
Or am I not walking with You?
Truly, I don't know.
However it is
I'm frightened, troubled, baffled.
Everything I do
Is with such fierce effort.
All my emotions are wire-crossed.
When others laugh, I cry.
When others run, I stumble.
When others sleep, I lie in darkness
Counting minutes, then hours.
I reach for Your hand
Until my fingers grow numb
But You give no response.
What's wrong, Lord?
How have I failed?
Don't You love me anymore?

DON'T YOU LOVE ME ANYMORE?

God, why do You turn from me
In my time of desperate need?
I have prayed and pleaded, O God.
I wake in the night with tears
Streaming down my face.
Why do You reject me
When You *promised* to deliver me?
Are You too busy to hear me?
Are You too busy to help me?
It's such a simple thing for You to help.
"You are forever, and Your years never end."
Does it matter to You about me?
Lord, don't You love me anymore?

LIKE A LONELY TREE

O God
On this cold January morning
I am like a lonely tree
On a distant mountaintop—
Leafless, brittle, trembling.
Howling winds twist me mercilessly.
How long must I wait, dear Lord
For the brilliant sun
To melt the heavy-packed snow?
And when will You prove
To my aching heart
That one lonely tree
On top of a snow-covered mountain
Has purpose wherever it grows!
As I stand against the forceful elements
I pray. I watch. I wait.
I long to see streams of water
Flowing down soft, rolling hills.
Perhaps I shall be productive again
When the long, long winter is past.

BY YOU, DEAR GOD

To be tattered and torn
Bit by bit, day-in, day-out
Or to be shattered totally
Like a crystal goblet
Flung fiercely against a giant rock.
To know the brutal intensity
Of pain and despair.
O God
How unbearable it seems
How intolerable as it happens.

But finally, finally
To stand against the storm
To stretch with the strain
To accept the pain
With a measure of quiet hope.
To look beyond the intrusion
And above the confusion
To catch a glimpse of rainbow
In an ocean of tears . . .

O great God
This is to trace at last
Your guiding hand—
To sense Your gentle touch.
This is to know Your presence—
More precious than understanding—
To know Your compassion
Persists through the darkest night.

This is to walk courageously on
In the midst of a desolate wilderness.
This is to be loved
To be held
To be kept
By the Sustainer of the universe.

To be loved
To be held
To be kept
By You, dear God
By You!

I KNOW YOU BEST

God
So often I have
Seen and heard You
Between smiles
And singing
And laughter.
But I am beginning to see
I learn to know You best
Between sobs.

AT SUCH TIMES

God, there are times
In the midst of heartache and heartbreak
When there is no comfort, no solace
Anywhere at all.
There are times
When in my crumbling state of mind
I feel I can no longer endure—
Not for a day, not even an hour.
It is at such times, O God
That I draw heavily
Upon Your unfathomable love.
At such times I implore
Your transforming peace.
At such times I live
By the power and promises
Of a Father who cares infinitely more
Than I can begin to grasp or comprehend.
Today, dear God, is a "such time."

GIVE US A TOKEN

Lord, today as I sit quietly
By my husband's hospital bed
All the rooms of my heart
Hold nothing but dark closets—
Musty and air-tight.
Please open another door
Or build another room in my heart
With wide-open windows
So I can glimpse the blue sky
Smell the fragrances of spring
And hear at least one chirping bird—
A token, dear Lord
That Your love is never-ending
Even when we're tempted to ask
"Don't You love us anymore?"

LOST ARGUMENT

I read this morning
Your direct and piercing question
To the ancient Job:
"Do you still want to argue
With the Almighty?
Or will you yield?"
With thoughtful heart
I read Job's wise reply:
"I am nothing. . . .
How could I find the answers?
I lay my hand upon my mouth in silence."
You know so well what I do, God.
I continue to argue with You
As though I were in charge.
As though I could solve my own dilemma.
Finally in the end, broken and defeated
I yield to You, and then—peace.
Forgive me, dear God
For so foolishly ending
Where I should have begun.

FOOLISH CHILD

O God
Why do You play
A threatening game
Of hide-and-seek with me
When I know You are there?

Foolish child
It is not hide-and-seek.
It is only SEEK.
Seek Me with all your heart.
You will surely find Me.
Never do I play games
With My cherished children.

RELENTLESS

God, You are relentless.
I have yielded
Everything to You—
Everything but one small exception—
An exception so small
I'm truly amazed
You would even take notice.
Yet it is invariably
To that one small exception
That You keep bringing me
Back, and back, and back.
Why does it matter so much to You?

My child
Why does it matter so much to you?

ESPECIALLY TODAY

O my Father!
Every day of my life I need You
But somehow today
My need is especially great.
With all my heart
I ask that I might not be swept away
By overwhelming temptation.
You know my deep longing to be released
From the agony of this debilitating illness.
Empower me not to give in to the pain
The loneliness, the long stretches of night.

I remember, dear Lord
How You knelt in agony and torment
Knowing how soon You would endure
The cruel and awful suffering of the Cross.
It was for me You suffered, dear Lord.
It was for me.

So keep me from falling prey
To self-pity and compromise.
I am so often tempted, God—so often.
I am reluctant to make solemn promises—
Promises too often easily broken.
So I simply ask You to hold me steady
Hour by hour, moment by moment.
Give me the moral courage
(Even through my faltering)
To learn from You the liberating secret

Of a peaceful, patient heart.
I read in Your Word
That when my patience is in full bloom
I will be whole and complete.
I will, in fact, be ready for anything.
What greater comfort could I ever experience
Than to be ready for anything?
I need it today, Lord.
Especially today.

WHY DO YOU ASK?

O God
My doctrine
Is so solid and sound.
Why is my living
So often sullied and soft?

Child of My constant love
Why do you ask?
You know the answer so well.

EVERY VALLEY EXALTED

Sometimes, Lord
It seems as though
You are the God of the hills
But not of the valleys.
For these past months
I have lived in a dark, lonely valley.
But then I remember Your promise
That every valley shall be exalted.
God, help me to persevere, to endure
Until my personal valley
Is gloriously exalted.

WHY?

Right now, dear God
I am so at peace with You
I want nothing but this moment
Exactly as it is.
But why are the distractions so many
And the moments so few?

I NEEDED THIS EXPERIENCE

O God
This year has been so difficult
So humiliating and painful.
Not only have I failed
I have *utterly* failed.
How confident I felt at the beginning!
I was so sure of financial success.
So sure of praise and commendation.
But all that has come
From my self-implemented project
Is loss and rejection.

And yet, dear Lord
You knew so much better than I
That I needed this experience
To show me my gross indifference toward You.
I was not asking for wisdom
Or seeking Your help in making decisions.
I was manipulative, evasive, arrogant
Glued to the center of my own little world.
Then everything crashed around me
And I began to discover afresh, dear God
That no success in all the world
No glamour, no glitter
Can even begin to compensate
For not having You.

SECRET RESERVATIONS

Forgive me, dear Lord
For singing the hymns of consecration
So lustily this Sunday morning.
With my head held high
I sang at the top of my voice
Aware that at the bottom of my heart
There were so many secret reservations.

Lord,
Teach Me Well

PLEASE TEACH ME WELL

God, it is drastically important
That the pain of this past year
Is not wasted.
How tragic it would be
To suffer so much
And gain so little.
What I *must* learn in my pain
Is that it is always leading
To something far beyond
What I can see in the shadows.
I *must* learn that You are not reckless
Or careless or cruel.
You are *for* me, and always
In some way, at some time
There is Your "nevertheless afterward."
I *must* learn that there is never a moment
When You are not worthy of praise.
Bad things happen
But there is only goodness in You.
I *must* learn that when my heart is broken
You are able to break my impatience, my pride
My carelessness and selfishness.
All of this I *must* learn.
O God, teach me well . . . teach me well.
It is drastically important
That the pain is not wasted.

WAIT QUIETLY

Lord, today my heart cringes
As I read Your Word:
"It is good that we should both hope
And quietly wait
For the salvation of the Lord."
God, I have been waiting, waiting, waiting.
How endlessly long I have been waiting!
Only You, Lord, can teach me to wait *quietly*.

IN A SUPERMARKET

Lord
While making my grocery list today
I suddenly began to wonder
If there was any possible way
I could serve You in a supermarket
Crowded with weary, stressful shoppers.
I seemed to hear You whisper
"A hundred lonely people need your smile."
Now as I hurriedly restock my shelves
After two hours of heavy shopping
I remember Your conservative estimate.
Surely I smiled more than a hundred times!
Thank You, Lord, for showing me
How to serve You in a supermarket
While pushing a cart loaded with groceries.

THE DARKEST OF NIGHTS

I know it is true, dear Lord
That on the darkest of nights
Every glittering star
Continues to shine at Your command.
And now, dear God
On this, the darkest of all my nights
Empower me to let my light shine
In obedience to Your command.

EXCLUSIVELY

Lord
I am so sick of belonging to things
So weary of belonging to people.
Help me to open my heart
To the peace that comes
From belonging exclusively to You.

SO SLOWLY

Lord
I seem to grow so slowly
So *very* slowly.
So thank You for reminding me
That never has a Master Musician
Composed a lasting symphony
In an hour.

FRUSTRATION TO PEACE

Everything went wrong today—
Just everything.
Big things, little things
So many unforeseen problems
So many unanticipated demands.
My carefully planned agenda
Was so splattered with interruptions
I could scarcely read what I'd written.
Even before the end of the day
I was stricken with total fatigue.
The whole day was a nuisance
With very few moments of calm.
But just a little while before dinner
As I stood in the kitchen grating carrots
I suddenly felt my husband's gentle touch.
He turned me around and held me close.
Then very tenderly he took my hand
And placed it into the hand of God.
Suddenly a beautiful thing happened:
All my fruitless frustration
Turned to quiet peace.
Lord, thank You. Thank You so much!

LIFE'S WHYS

Lord
If You were to answer
All of life's whys
Surely You would have started
With Your servant Job.
Instead, Your determined goal for Job
Was unrivaled loyalty and trust.
And so, dear God
As achingly difficult as it often is
Enable me to trust You
With such total abandonment
That You will hear no complaining
When I hear no explaining.

LOST SHEPHERD

Sometimes, Lord
In my groping effort to find You
I have reversed the parable
Of the Shepherd and the sheep.
In my distorted concept
The Shepherd has been lost
And the sheep have trudged down
Dangerous mountain cliffs to find him.
How sadly prone I am to forget
That I would not be searching for You
If You were not first wanting me.
Let me remember always, Lord
How foolish it is
To stumble through darkness
Searching for You
When I need only to surrender
To Your search for me.

BE MY TEACHER

Whenever I am the speaker
At a mountain retreat
I have a secret longing
To stay at the top of the mountain
Just rejoicing in You, dear God.
But always You remind me
That the mountaintop experience
Is simply to teach me
How to live consistently in the valley.
You remind me, too, that life is reality
Not sheer ecstasy and delight.
The sooner I learn that truth
The more productive my life will be.
Be my Teacher, dear Lord
But please be patient with me.
There are times when I struggle
To work up to an F.

GOD, WHY DO YOU HIDE?

O God
Why do You hide from me
When I need You so much?
Why do You make it so difficult
For me to find You
When I know You are there?
When You have given me
Great and glorious promises
Why are none of them fulfilled?
When loneliness overwhelms me
Where is Your hand?
When I am depleted with fatigue
Where is Your rest?
O God, why do You hide from me?

Child of many questions
How can I answer
When you never stop asking?

LOSE ME IN YOU

O dear God
Lose me in You
Until I find myself anew!
When You are my permanent address
Changing phone numbers
Won't matter.

AN ALLELUIA

It was Augustine who said
"A Christian should be an Alleluia
From head to foot."
Too often, Lord, I am a funeral dirge
Spreading gloom and pessimism
Mixed with worry and fear.
Put a new song in my heart, God.
Give me a singing trust.
Remold and remake me
Into Your personal alleluia.

TOTALLY CONSISTENT

O God
Stretch my soul
Until my experience
Matches my knowledge—
Until what I *know* to do
Is totally consistent
With what I actually do
In obedience to Your commands.

EASTER MORNING

Lord, on this bell-chiming Easter
So fragrant with spring
So vibrant with colorful clusters
Please walk with me
Arm-in-arm
Down my personal Emmaus Road.
But, Lord
Unlike the early disciples
May I instantly know
From the very first step
That I'm walking
With my Risen Lord.

WORST—BEST

O God
It is difficult for me to think coherently
To pray with any kind of sequence today.
I am so weary, so worn, so fragmented.
But, Lord, perhaps to Your ears
Sometimes my worst praying
Is really my best.
I trust so . . . I trust so.
One thing I do know:
All my desire is before You!

TIME TO ACT

Lord
Today You clearly told me
To get on with the job—
The task I've been evading
The task You've told me
Countless times to tackle.
You reminded me forcefully
That I've been praying long enough.
It's time now to ACT!
As I obey You will reward me
With peace and spiritual prosperity.
Again I see that obedience
Is always the thing with You.

DESCENDANT OF ADAM

Lord, at times of soaring victory
The Psalmist said he would sing to You
As long as he lived.
He said he would praise You
To his very last breath.
He said he would bless Your Name forever.
But, Lord, how well I remember
David's bitter complaints
During days of fear and despair.
He asked if You had forgotten to be gracious.
He asked if he had offended You.
He asked if Your mercy was gone forever.
As you forgave David's complaints
Lord, please forgive mine.
I too am a descendant of Adam!

DIVIDED HEART

Lord
I am so often tormented
By my lack of clear direction—
So often disturbed
By my divided heart.

I am like a little child
Who wants to rock her doll
And jump rope at the same time.
I want to obey You in part
If I can choose the areas of obedience.
I want to be real except at those moments
When compromise is more appealing.
I want to be half-motivated
And half-satisfied with things as they are.
I want to walk a straight path
If now and then I can enjoy
A few side trips into the far country.
I don't want to be a miserable sinner
But neither do I feel excited
About being a stoic saint.
I want to be partly Yours
And partly my own.

But in the secret chamber
Of my divided heart
I am so often disquieted
By the pointed question:
"Why do you so foolishly
Mix weeds with seeds?"

God
of All
Grace

MY DESTINY

O God
Despite my deep desire to please You
In the midst of confinement and pain
There are so many temptations
That hover like a thick cloud
Over all my honest efforts.
Is there ever an escape, dear God
From the subtle temptations
That accompany perpetual pain?
How can I avoid the clamoring thoughts
The weakness, the helplessness
The pricking irritations?
Then, dear God, there are the weary mornings
After sleepless nights.
The disturbing fears that cling so tightly.
How can I resist the "if onlys"
When the pain pierces with such intensity?

Over and over the question Why? creeps
    stealthily
Into the dark corners of my thoughts.
"Why *this*, dear God, when I long to serve You?"
"Why *this*, when in an instant You could make
    me well?"
And yet, dear God, I know I must stop
    brooding.
I must stop badgering.
You need not explain Your eternal purpose
In terms I can understand.

71

Help me to respond without murmuring
About Your method of molding me
For I can know with unshakable assurance
That my destiny is perfection
In the eternal presence of the living God.

ALL I WANT

Lord, now that You
Are all I have
I am suddenly, joyfully aware
That You are all I want!

HOW LONG IS EVERLASTING?

O dear God
How long will You ignore me?
How long must I continue to weep before You?
Will You forever keep silent
When I seek Your face?
Surely You know my desperation
And yet I cannot arouse Your attention.
Must I continually stumble
Through dense forests and dark valleys?
Does it matter to You about me?
I don't understand, Lord.
In the past You so lavishly blessed me.
Have I offended You?
Are there false motives that I cannot trace?
Are You searching me out?
O Lord, I cannot endure the thought
That You no longer love me.
Hear my cry, dear God.
Please speak to me.

Listen, dear child
Quietly listen.
I have loved you
With an everlasting love.
How long is everlasting?

WRONG QUESTION

My faithful God
I see afresh this morning
The grave error of my question
"Don't You love me anymore?"
I ought always to ask instead
"How can You love me so continually
With such immeasurable love?"

GOD OF ALL GRACE

God of all grace
Please bring an end
To this hideous nightmare.
Lift the heavy weight of despondency.
Remove the confusion
The brokenness
The crushing anxiety
The awful pain.
How I long to sense the joy
Of Your healing touch.
You are a God of integrity
A God of infinite kindness.
Surely it cannot be true
That You no longer love me.

THE PROMISE
(2 Samuel 22:29, TLB)

And the Lord will lighten my darkness . . .

O Lord, how I needed to read this promise
In Your Word this very day.
You will lighten my darkness.
You will *personally* do it.
I cannot, nor can my family.
My friends cannot
Nor can the one dearest to me.
You alone can lighten my darkness.
Though it is pitch black
Though clouds pile heavy and high
Though thunder roars
Though I see only confusion
You will lighten my darkness.
My hope is in You.
I look for You. I wait for You.
Nothing will prevent it.
You will lighten my darkness.

NEVER TOO LATE

Sometimes, dear Lord
You work so slowly!

Tell Me, dear child
Have I ever been too late?

YOU PROMISED ME

Lord, just today I read again
The words of the prophet, Ezra.
Long years ago he prayed
"You have done what You promised
For You are always true to Your word."
My dear Lord, look into my heart.
Listen to my repeated plea.
You promised me, Lord
You promised me.
You promised deliverance
From crushing defeat.
You promised Your peace
In my aching despair.
You promised release
From agonizing pain.
I've waited so long . . . so long.
Still I cling tenaciously
To this solemn truth:
You are always true to Your word.
I trust You, dear God.
I expect to pray as Ezra prayed:
"You have done what You promised
For You are always true to Your word."

ACCEPT—EXPECT

My Father
Empower me to *accept*
All You have promised
And to *expect*
Every promise fulfilled.
May I never forget
How completely I am in Your hands.

I PROMISE YOU

My Father
How You will send Your help
I don't know.
But as certain as You are Love
Your help will come!
As surely as You keep Your word
You will supply my need.
I don't know what to do
But my eyes are on You.
You have said
"I promise you."

DAY OF REJOICING

Lord, all day long
We've been laughing and singing.
We've been shouting and praising.
After weeks and months
Of waiting and pleading
You have wonderfully answered our prayers.
Our hearts are filled with unspeakable joy.
You promised that those
Who sow in tears
Shall reap in joy.
It is happening, dear Lord
To us . . . to *us!*

VERY DIFFERENT

Lord
Please put me
Where the talents and gifts
You've given me
Can be best used.
Put me, I pray
Where I can best serve You.
This is the deep longing
Of my heart.

My child
I will put you
Where you can best glorify Me.
This may be very different
Than all your present dreams.

ONE STUPENDOUS THING

O dear God
If You love me at all
(And I want to believe You do)
I beg You to do one stupendous thing
For my torn and bleeding heart:
Please dear Lord
Take the place
Of what You've taken away.
I cannot survive
I cannot endure
Unless You grant this request.

IMMEDIATELY

Dear Lord
I'm so tired of living
In my little cramped vessel—
So weary of dangling my feet in the water
But never stepping out of the boat.
I want to walk the waves with You
Just as Peter did.
True, he took only a few steps
Before losing his courage
But at least he was heading toward You.
Lord, I'm coming, too!
If I begin to falter or sink
I trust You to catch me
Just as You caught Peter.
Remember, Lord?
You caught him *immediately*.

I'M HERE

God, I cannot see You
But I wait for You.

My child
I can see you
And I'm here.

I NEED YOUR POWER

Lord God
I so desperately need Your power.
Not only to *sustain* me
In times of overwhelming trouble
But to *restrain* me
In times of overwhelming temptation.

THREE UNALTERABLE TRUTHS

Lord, through the years
Of walking hand-in-hand with You
I have learned three unalterable truths:
First, what You command me to do
You consistently expect me to do.
Never do You say, "Give the command a fair
   try."
Nor do You say, "Consider and then decide."
My natural weakness is never
An acceptable excuse.
Nor is my inability
To reach unreachable standards.
Rather, You tell me to *seek*
And then to *keep* Your commands.
Second, all of Your commands
Are always for my ultimate good.
"Obey Me," Your Word says
"So that I can do for you
All the wonderful things I promised. . . ."
"In the keeping of My Word
There is great reward."
Third, whatever You command me to do
You fully enable me to do.
As You give light to reveal a command
So You give grace to fulfill it.
Your divine energy is always at my disposal.
The choice to obey is always mine.
The power to obey is always Yours.

HOW WILL I KNOW?

Lord, I long to know You
So personally, so intimately
That I shall never
Leave an impression of myself
But only of You.
But, Lord, how will I know
When I am loving You
That personally, that intimately?

My child
Your life will bear fruit.

FREE CHOICE

My Lord
Because You have given me
The irrevocable power of free choice
You will not force me
To do something
I selfishly don't want to do.
But I have made
A grave and painful discovery:
You can certainly
Make me wish I had done it.

MANY EXCUSES

Lord, I'm sorry, so sorry
I neglected to do
What You asked of me today.
My intentions were honorable
But the hours slipped by so quickly
And—well, there honestly wasn't time.
However, I did make three friendly phone calls.
I trust that was just as good.

Child of many excuses
When you reject my specific request
Nothing else is ever "just as good."

DEAD GIVEAWAY

O dear God
My heart overflows
With proclamations of joy!
You are so good
So faithful
Your loving-kindness is so great.
I long for my continual gratitude
To be a dead giveaway
Of my deepening love for You.

A God
Who
Acts

SOUL STRUGGLE

Her uncontrollable sobs know no respite.
"What is wrong with me"
She stammers convulsively
"That love has passed me by?
Am I so ugly, so stupidly plain?
Am I some kind of an oddity?
Doesn't God love me anymore?"

Lord, there are times when she hides
Behind a sophisticated facade
But today she is not pretending.
In her deep loneliness
There are no words to comfort her.
You alone can release her
From her shadowy world.
You alone can break the bleakness
And produce the firm conviction
Of Your measureless love.
Lord, my part in her soul's struggle
Is to reach for her hand.
Your part is to reach for her heart.

MOMENT BY MOMENT

Today, dear Lord
I asked You how I could know
If my surrender was complete.
I asked if I had truly yielded
All that I am and all that I have.
Simply but directly You answered
"How is it with you now, this moment?
Settle it each moment
And you won't need to ask."

TWO QUESTIONS

O Lord
Where is the God
Who loves me?

My faltering one
Where is the child
Who trusts Me?

THE PROMISE

O dear God, I continue to believe
Your personal promise still stands
Though every quivering emotion within
Shouts that it will be broken.
I am claiming Your help through the wilderness
Despite every frightening shadow and vale.
Often you do the most
When You seem to do the least.
Sometimes secretly
Sometimes quietly
Often slowly
But always most certainly
You are true to Your word.
And so, my Lord
Though I am weak, weary, and worn
Help me not to despair.
You see me, You hear me.
You know I am depending utterly
Upon Your unblemished integrity.
Surely You will keep Your word.

O GOD . . . MY GOD

O God . . . *My* God
Though You now seem totally hidden
I am clinging to You hopefully
Even confidently.
Someday, some way, You will make
All You are now permitting
Blessedly clear.
With fixed purpose, dear God
I am determined to wait, to trust
To rely upon Your faithfulness.
Despite the drain and strain
I anticipate new perspectives
And fresh depths of insight
Into all that is now so mysterious.
O God, in ways unanticipated
You are teaching me the great truth
Of Samuel Rutherford's words:
"I see that grace grows best in winter."
Thank You, dear God
Thank You for that!

WATCHMAN,
WHAT OF THE NIGHT?

Today I read again
The piercing question
In the book of Isaiah:
"Watchman, what of the night?"
I too have a question, my Lord:
In the darkness of my nights
When pain permeates my body
When sleep evades me
When fatigue overwhelms me
When I cannot run or hide
Will You be my night watchman?
And when in fear and desperation
I ask, "Watchman, what of my night?"
Please let me hear Your gentle words:
"Joy cometh in the morning."

UNDENIABLE TRUTH

God, forgive me.
I am suddenly aware
That for many months
I have been more occupied
With my personal pain and loss
Than I have been with You.
I know it is true:
You are not obligated to explain
My crushing blows or my aching void.
Help me to trust You for who You are
Regardless of what You permit.
I acknowledge Your Sovereignty, God
But I long for You to burn
Into every fiber of my being
The undeniable truth
That throughout all eternity
You are a loving, caring
And forever faithful Sovereign.

WISTFUL LONGING

O God
Where is the strong assurance
I knew so well a short time ago?
Why is my heart suddenly so empty
And my thoughts so dull?
Why am I tormented with pain
And tortured with doubt?
What has corroded my trust?
Please, dear Lord
In Your loving-kindness
Break into my cloud of confusion
And free me as You would have done
Had I touched the hem of Your garment
When You walked on earth.
I look to You with wistful longing.
I wait for Your gentle touch.

I AM SURE OF YOU

Lord, I was sure of my faith
Just long enough
To watch it collapse.
Now I am sure of *You*
And You will not collapse.

OVERWHELMED

Lord, I'm overwhelmed
By my inadequacies and failures.
So often I'm ashamed
To face my friends.
I continually sense
That they look down on me.
It's my greatest problem.

Foolish child
Your greatest problem
Is that you don't
Look up to Me.

I OFTEN FORGET

God
In the night's darkness
When sleep is evasive
I try with some semblance of clarity
To talk to You.
But I am troubled, dear Lord
After sleep finally beckons me
For by morning I often have forgotten what I
    prayed.

Never fear, weary child.
Though you forget
I always remember.

SUDDEN AWE

My face wind-lashed
With stinging sand
Alone I trudge the beach
Filled with sudden awe
That You, O God
Are mightier by far
Than all the breakers
Pounding on the seashores
Of the world.

"GREAT STIRRER-UP"

Lord, Frank Laubach was right
When he spoke of You
As the "Great Stirrer-Up."
Invariably You are determined
To stir me out of my lethargy
And self-satisfaction.
When once again You have aroused me
And restored my sensitivity
To the plan You have ordained for me
You amaze me with delightful surprises
I would never have discovered on my own—
Never in a thousand years!
What a true description of You, God—
The "Great Stirrer-Up."

IT'S CHRISTMAS!

It's Christmas!

Sing!
Rejoice!
Celebrate!

Let God create in you
Colorful explosions
Of joy and excitement.
Smile away fears, push away tears.
Out with pretense, in with praise.

It's Christmas!

Open your heart to light
To trust, to love, to hope.
Awaken slumbering memories
Stir up stupendous dreams
Anticipate surprises
Open your arms wide.

It's Christmas!

Time for candles and cards
For carols and cookies
For brightly lit trees
With the fragrance of pine.
Time to hug and hold

To think and thank
Time to greet the world
With the Good News.

It's Christmas!

Thank God for life
Thank Him for the manger
For the splintered cross
For the empty tomb.
Thank Him for His only Son
The Savior of the world.

Shout!
Laugh!
Share!
Care!

And say to God
On Christmas morning:
"I entrust myself anew
To You."

THE MINUTES

God
It is early morning
And I begin this rain-splashed day
By offering You every minute.
I am confident, Lord
That if You have control
Of all my minutes
There is not a single reason
For me to fear the next hour
Or the next
Or the next.

I DARE TO BELIEVE

"Out of the depths I cry to You, O Lord."
On this day of remorse and turmoil
The Psalmist's cry is my cry.
Trembling, crumbling, out of the depths I cry.
And yet, in the throes of my anguish, O God
I dare to believe
You see my groping and grasping.
You hear my sighs and sobs.
I dare to believe
You can break through the emotional blockades
You can rebuild my broken dreams.
Though my words seem drenched with
    presumption
To those who march with illusive courage
I dare to believe
Your love is unquenchable
Your faithfulness is inexhaustible.
I dare to believe
You delight to draw me to Yourself
You long to silence my desperate cry.
I dare to believe
I will yet hear Your gentle words
"I am your Father.
Come home."

Weeping child
It is true
That I am your Father.
Now dare to believe
You are *home.*

FALSE CONCLUSION

Lord, may I never surrender
To the false conclusion
That You have no more for me
Than what I already have.

I READ YOUR HEART

O God
I find it so difficult to praise You
In the throes of crushing pain.
I try, but thoughts twirl in confusion
And words refuse to formulate.
In my aching weariness
I cannot even read a Psalm of praise.
Do You understand, dear Lord?

My very own child
You need not fear
I read your heart!

I TRUST YOU

Lord, it was on an April morning
So many years ago
That You said to me so clearly
"Trust Me and you won't be disappointed."
Having heard You on that special morning
I simply cannot "unhear" you now.
I can't forget that morning
Nor do I think You want me to.
Because You live in an eternal Now
Your words are just as relevant today
As they were that long-ago morning.
I *trust* You. You will not disappoint me!

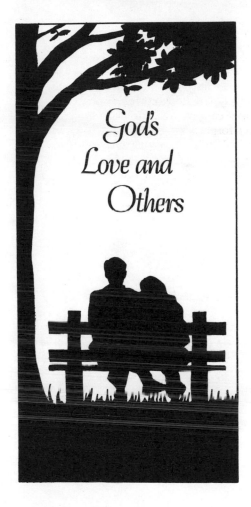

God's
Love and
Others

A BEAUTIFUL WORD

O God, our quarrel this early morning
Was so senseless, so demolishing.
We slashed each other with sarcasm.
We said cruel things to each other—
Things we honestly didn't mean.
I know I am far too sensitive, Lord.
Touchy might be a more accurate word.
My inclination is always first to brood
And then to inflict the silent treatment
Waiting for my husband to make amends.

But when I think of our solid marriage
Of forty-three productive years
One truth is deeply ingrained within me.
There is no hurt worth clinging to
When we love each other as we do.
Lord, *forgiveness* is a beautiful word.
Tonight when my husband comes home from
    work
May I be the first to forgive
The minute he unlocks the door.

BROKEN CHAINS

"I'm no longer smoking"
She said to me triumphantly.
"By sheer will-power I'm free.
I simply determined
I would not be chained to a habit."
That's why I was so surprised
To see her smoking again
After six or seven months.
God, it occurs to me
That broken chains are often mendable.
Another pertinent reminder
That *purification* is more needed
Than determination.

THE GREAT INVESTMENT

I praise You, dear Lord
For teaching my husband and me
To make friends with the money
You have entrusted to us.
We have so little to invest
In stocks and bonds
But so much to invest
In lonely, empty lives.
And, Lord, the rate of interest
Is enormously high.
In fact, as we continue to invest
The interest goes up and up and up!

LONELY HEART

O God
How I long to encourage her—
To say or do something
To renew her shattered hope.
She told me that when her husband left
You seemed to leave, too.
Panic seized her, and dread.
A sense of futility.
"If God is a God of love," she sobbed
"How could He let this happen?"
Despairing, she trudges
Through each dreary day
Too unsure to start afresh
Too confused right now to pray.
Lord, create within her
A deep longing for You.
If she turns from You
As her husband turned from her
She will be twice bereft.
God, I will walk with her
On her winding journey toward recovery
But You alone can heal her empty heart.

WELCOME HOME

Dear lonely old man!
Just a bit eccentric, perhaps.
Friendly whenever he had a chance to be
But certainly nobody thought he was stimulating.
When he walked he was always alone.
In church he sat alone, too.
Always near the rear of the sanctuary.
That's why I was so surprised
To see so many at his memorial service.
Some who would not have crossed the street
To greet him while he still lived.
Lord, he must have loved his entrance to
    heaven.
Never before had anyone stood in line
Just to welcome him home!

HURTING HEART

How pathetically she attempts
To be courageous and strong
Despite her desperate need
To express her deep grief.
She solemnly promised her husband
She would stand firm
When his death parted them.
She said, "I want to keep my promise.
He would trust me to do that."
And so she smiles while her lips quiver—
And her longing heart weeps.
Soon, perhaps, the pushed-back tears will come.
I pray so, Lord. Oh, I pray so!
But right now, please hold her hurting heart
As a mother holds a hurting child.

REGRET

After she refilled our coffee cups
The third or fourth time
My husband praised her
For her efficiency as a waitress.
She flashed a grateful smile.
"Oh, sir, you've made my day!"

Lord, when we left the restaurant
I was so sorry I hadn't found a way
To tell her *You* could make her *life*.

INDICTMENT

O God
When I think of Your
Tremendous goodness to us
Your continual poured-out blessings
Suddenly I am overwhelmed
With a convicting thought:
Everything You do
For my husband and me
All Your love and kindness
So lavishly bestowed
Become an indictment
Unless we willingly
Allow each blessing
To flow through us to others.
All Your abundance
Must constantly be on the move
Or we will stagnate
In a sea of plenty.

HE'S LATE AGAIN

Lord, he's late again.
It's raining so hard
And traffic is always heavy
At this time of day.
I never feel secure
With those huge trucks
On the freeway.
Could a tire have gone flat?
Did he stop to see someone?
Surely he would have called.
I wonder . . . didn't he feel well
When he left this morning?
I remember how gently he held me
When he kissed me good-bye.
Did he think something might happen?
When we prayed at the table
I asked You to keep him safe.
Did You hear me, Lord?
Dinner is getting cold.
Should I reheat the oven?
Wait! I think I hear the car door slam.
I do! Beautiful sound! He's home!

Why does he do this to me, Lord?
Doesn't he understand my stress?
Doesn't he stop to think
I could have a heart attack?

Keep me from exploding, Lord.
My husband is home
And that's all that matters.
I do love him so!

RIGHT FOR EACH OTHER

Thank You, dear God
That my husband and I
Are as right for each other
In the dull and daily routine
As we are in the quiet darkness.

THANKSGIVING DAY DREAM

On this fragrant, frosty Thanksgiving Day
The huge turkey browns beautifully
In our king-size oven.
The tender yams are evenly candied;
The corn souffle is beginning to bubble;
The congealed salad is ready to unmold.
The homemade bread with its crunchy texture
Is wrapped in foil for reheating.
The ice cubes are bagged in plastic;
The relishes are artistically arranged
On a round crystal plate.
The pumpkin pies are still slightly warm.
Fresh yellow chrysanthemums
Grace the long, colorful table.
The house glistens and shines.
My makeup is evenly applied. . . .

So, dear family
How about settling down
In our favorite chairs
For an hour of relaxation
Before our guests arrive!

Lord, I dream of this happening
Some ethereal Thanksgiving Day!

FORGIVE MY CRITICAL ATTITUDE

Lord
Forgive my critical attitude—
My judgmental spirit.
It is true that I saw my friend fall again
But not once did I consider
The countless times she did *not* fall
Though she was severely tempted.
Help me to bind myself more closely
And more lovingly to her.
May she know that I continue to believe
In Your victory in her life
Despite any sudden barrier of defeat.
May I redouble my love and vigilance
Until she is renewed and restored—
Until she is able to give to others
The support she herself has received.

CHRISTMAS GRATITUDE

Lord
As I stand at the kitchen sink
Mixing batter for Christmas cookies
The scent of spicy pine
Permeates our house.
Already everyone is rushing in our town!
I remember that it started years ago
When the startled shepherds
Came with haste
To find the newborn Baby.

Dear God
As I bake enormous batches of cookies
This beautiful Christmas season
I pray for sufficient strength
To go with haste
To the frightened and lonely
To the worn and weary
To those without courage and hope.
Lord, may each batch of cookies
Be mixed with love—
Not just mine, but Yours!

Right now, dear God
With flour smudging my face
And dough clinging to my fingers
I praise You with all my heart
For loving us enough
To give the very best—
The gift of Your only begotten Son.

THE GRIEF YOU ENDURE

God, how can he fail You so unashamedly?
How can he disobey so excessively?
How can he turn his back on You
And blatantly continue his own defiant way?
How can he excuse his gross selfishness
His pride, his stubborn resistance?
How can he so totally ignore You
And pretend that all is well?
How my heart aches, dear God
For the grief You endure for him.

My troubled child
Does anyone ache for you?

I REALLY KNEW

I have discovered, Lord
That some hospital visitors
Are extremely insensitive to timing.
I remember the woman who came to visit
When my husband was at his very worst.
The doctor had just said to me
"We are puzzled. Your husband is very ill
And we have not found the cause of his illness."
The woman listened with a broad smile.
She was in exuberant health.
Never had she been a patient in a hospital.
I wondered as I looked at her
If she had ever suffered great pain.
"Remember," she said triumphantly
"God never gives us more than we can bear!"
Lord, I knew what she said was true.
I really *knew.*
And yet at that moment, dear God
I would so much rather have heard it from You.

A BETTER WAY?

Today I saw two of them—
Little black bugs
With hard, shiny shells.
The tough shells guarded them
From my newspaper attack.

Lord, sometimes I think
My husband and I
Need shells like that
When we are attacking each other.
Or do You have a better way?

THOUGH IT TAKES A LIFETIME

Lord—
Sometimes I wonder
How two imperfect people
Can possibly build
A perfect marriage.
And then I stop wondering
For I know they cannot.

But this they can do:
They can invite You
The perfect One
To share day by day
In their togetherness.
Gently, carefully
You will nurture them.
You will transform
Their imperfections.

Though it takes a lifetime
Their marriage will bear
Luscious fruit . . . like a tree
Planted along a riverbank—
And all that they do
Shall prosper.

FORTY-THREE YEARS

Forty-three years of marriage.
That's a lot of years!
Somewhere in a box of treasured things
I still have the postcard
I sent to my parents
While we were on our honeymoon.
I saved it because of its rare combination
Of humor and naïveté:
"Bliss! Nothing but bliss!
Day after day of uninterrupted bliss!"
That sentimental bit of melodrama
Was written after we had given our marriage
The long, enduring test of   eleven days.
We had a lot to learn!

One thing is certain:
Whatever marriage was meant to be
It wasn't meant to be easy.
It's different when you're married.
You're accountable to each other.
You're making a life investment
In a permanent relationship.
At least that was our personal decision
Right from the very beginning.
True, sometimes I'm plodding
When I'd rather soar.
Or I'm submerged in soapsuds
When I'd rather be sunning on a sandy shore.
But when it comes right down to it

I wouldn't trade my lot
With any woman who ever lived. . . .

We lie side by side in the darkness.
Our fingers touch, our weary bodies relax.
Before we go to sleep my husband says
With beautiful gentleness
"I want you to know
I'm lying here loving you."

Forty-three years are a lot of years.
Lord, thank You for every one!

Other Living Books Best-sellers

THE ANGEL OF HIS PRESENCE by Grace Livingston Hill. This book captures the romance of John Wentworth Stanley and a beautiful young woman whose influence causes John to reevaluate his well-laid plans for the future. 07-0047 $2.95.

ANSWERS by Josh McDowell and Don Stewart. In a question-and-answer format, the authors tackle sixty-five of the most-asked questions about the Bible, God, Jesus Christ, miracles, other religions, and creation. 07-0021 $3.95.

THE BEST CHRISTMAS PAGEANT EVER by Barbara Robinson. A delightfully wild and funny story about what happens to a Christmas program when the "Horrible Herdman" brothers and sisters are miscast in the roles of the biblical Christmas story characters. 07-0137 $2.50.

BUILDING YOUR SELF-IMAGE by Josh McDowell. Here are practical answers to help you overcome your fears, anxieties, and lack of self-confidence. Learn how God's higher image of who you are can take root in your heart and mind. 07-1395 $3.95.

THE CHILD WITHIN by Mari Hanes. The author shares insights she gained from God's Word during her own pregnancy. She identifies areas of stress, offers concrete data about the birth process, and points to God's sure promises that he will "gently lead those that are with young." 07-0219 $2.95.

COME BEFORE WINTER AND SHARE MY HOPE by Charles R. Swindoll. A collection of brief vignettes offering hope and the assurance that adversity and despair are temporary setbacks we can overcome! 07-0477 $5.95.

DARE TO DISCIPLINE by James Dobson. A straightforward, plainly written discussion about building and maintaining parent/child relationships based upon love, respect, authority, and ultimate loyalty to God. 07-0522 $3.50.

DAVID AND BATHSHEBA by Roberta Kells Dorr. This novel combines solid biblical and historical research with suspenseful storytelling about men and women locked in the eternal struggle for power, governed by appetites they wrestle to control. 07-0618 $4.95.

FOR MEN ONLY edited by J. Allan Petersen. This book deals with topics of concern to every man: the business world, marriage, fathering, spiritual goals, and problems of living as a Christian in a secular world. 07-0892 $3.95.

FOR WOMEN ONLY by Evelyn and J. Allan Petersen. Balanced, entertaining, diversified treatment of all the aspects of womanhood. 07-0897 $4.95.

400 WAYS TO SAY I LOVE YOU by Alice Chapin. Perhaps the flame of love has almost died in your marriage. Maybe you have a good marriage that just needs a little "spark." Here is a book especially for the woman who wants to rekindle the flame of romance in her marriage; who wants creative, practical, useful ideas to show the man in her life that she cares. 07-0919 $2.95.

Other Living Books Best-sellers

GIVERS, TAKERS, AND OTHER KINDS OF LOVERS by Josh McDowell and Paul Lewis. This book bypasses vague generalities about love and sex and gets right to the basic questions: Whatever happened to sexual freedom? What's true love like? Do men respond differently than women? If you're looking for straight answers about God's plan for love and sexuality, this book was written for you. 07-1031 $2.95.

HINDS' FEET ON HIGH PLACES by Hannah Hurnard. A classic allegory of a journey toward faith that has sold more than a million copies! 07-1429 $3.95.

HOW TO BE HAPPY THOUGH MARRIED by Tim LaHaye. One of America's most successful marriage counselors gives practical, proven advice for marital happiness. 07-1499 $3.50.

JOHN, SON OF THUNDER by Ellen Gunderson Traylor. In this saga of adventure, romance, and discovery, travel with John—the disciple whom Jesus loved—down desert paths, through the courts of the Holy City, to the foot of the cross. Journey with him from his luxury as a privileged son of Israel to the bitter hardship of his exile on Patmos. 07-1903 $4.95.

LIFE IS TREMENDOUS! by Charlie "Tremendous" Jones. Believing that enthusiasm makes the difference, Jones shows how anyone can be happy, involved, relevant, productive, healthy, and secure in the midst of a high-pressure, commercialized society. 07-2184 $2.95.

LOOKING FOR LOVE IN ALL THE WRONG PLACES by Joe White. Using wisdom gained from many talks with young people, White steers teens in the right direction to find love and fulfillment in a personal relationship with God. 07-3825 $3.95.

LORD, COULD YOU HURRY A LITTLE? by Ruth Harms Calkin. These prayer-poems from the heart of a godly woman trace the inner workings of the heart, following the rhythms of the day and the seasons of the year with expectation and love. 07-3816 $2.95.

LORD, I KEEP RUNNING BACK TO YOU by Ruth Harms Calkin. In prayer-poems tinged with wonder, joy, humanness, and questioning, the author speaks for all of us who are groping and learning together what it means to be God's child. 07-3819 $3.50.

MORE THAN A CARPENTER by Josh McDowell. A hard-hitting book for people who are skeptical about Jesus' deity, his resurrection, and his claims on their lives. 07-4552 $2.95.

MOUNTAINS OF SPICES by Hannah Hurnard. Here is an allegory comparing the nine spices mentioned in the Song of Solomon to the nine fruits of the Spirit. A story of the glory of surrender by the author of *HINDS' FEET ON HIGH PLACES.* 07-4611 $3.95.

NOW IS YOUR TIME TO WIN by Dave Dean. In this true-life story, Dean shares how he locked into seven principles that enabled him to bounce back from failure to success. Read about successful men and women—from sports and entertainment celebrities to the ordinary people next door—and discover how you too can bounce back from failure to success! 07-4727 $2.95.

Other Living Books Best-sellers

THE POSITIVE POWER OF JESUS CHRIST by Norman Vincent Peale. All his life the author has been leading men and women to Jesus Christ. In this book he tells of his boyhood encounters with Jesus and of his spiritual growth as he attended seminary and began his world-renowned ministry. 07-4914 $4.50.

REASONS by Josh McDowell and Don Stewart. In a convenient question-and-answer format, the authors address many of the commonly asked questions about the Bible and evolution. 07-5287 $3.95.

ROCK by Bob Larson. A well-researched and penetrating look at today's rock music and rock performers, their lyrics, and their life-styles. 07-5686 $3.50.

THE STORY FROM THE BOOK. The full sweep of *The Book*'s content in abridged, chronological form, giving the reader the "big picture" of the Bible. 07-6677 $4.95.

SUCCESS: THE GLENN BLAND METHOD by Glenn Bland. The author shows how to set goals and make plans that really work. His ingredients of success include spiritual, financial, educational, and recreational balances. 07-6689 $3.50.

TELL ME AGAIN, LORD, I FORGET by Ruth Harms Calkin. You will easily identify with the author in this collection of prayer-poems about the challenges, peaks, and quiet moments of each day. 07-6990 $3.50.

THROUGH GATES OF SPLENDOR by Elisabeth Elliot. This unforgettable story of five men who braved the Auca Indians has become one of the most famous missionary books of all times. 07-7151 $3.95.

WAY BACK IN THE HILLS by James C. Hefley. The story of Hefley's colorful childhood in the Ozarks makes reflective reading for those who like a nostalgic journey into the past. 07-7821 $4.50.

WHAT WIVES WISH THEIR HUSBANDS KNEW ABOUT WOMEN by James Dobson. The best-selling author of *DARE TO DISCIPLINE* and *THE STRONG-WILLED CHILD* brings us this vital book that speaks to the unique emotional needs and aspirations of today's woman. An immensely practical, interesting guide. 07-7896 $3.50.